520 956 67 0

DQ676119

Sliders

Mini burgers

Sliders

Mini burgers

DAVID COWIE

NH
NEW HOLLAND

contents

Introduction

The first time I tried a slider I was in West Hollywood, with my wife and some friends. We'd stopped at a hotel for a drink and noticed everyone around us was eating little hamburgers. They looked amazing, so we had to try them as well. What a delicious discovery. Ever since that experience, I've been hooked on these mini burgers—known as sliders—and when I see them on any menu I have to order them to see how they look and how good they taste.

Sliders are great snacks. Because of their smaller size, you can serve a selection of meat, seafood and vegetarian sliders for everyone to sample. Dish them up with some of the tasty sides listed in the Sauces and Sides chapter. And liven up any of the recipes with a homemade sauce. These mini burgers make the perfect finger food when friends drop by, whether it's for a backyard barbecue or a fancy cocktail party.

And these little meals can become a part of the everyday family meal: they don't have to be unhealthy. Use lean mince or meat that's been trimmed of fat to make your patties, add plenty of fresh salad fillings and make some low-fat dressings. Put everything into a wholemeal or wholegrain bun and voila, you have a healthy meal.

Be as creative as you want and make these slider recipes your own. I hope you enjoy eating these delicious treats as much as you enjoy making them.

buns

THE BUNS

So what is a slider bun? Slider buns are your usual burger buns, just smaller. You can bake them yourself, if you're keen. I'm no baking expert, but I found that after a few attempts I started to get the hang of it and with a little passion and a little patience, I was able to create the perfect small slider bun.

If you are time-poor or don't want to go to that much trouble, have a look for slider buns at your local supermarket or bakery. You should be able to find small dinner rolls or brioche buns that can be easily used as slider buns. And mini hot dog rolls are also great as slider buns. Want to serve sliders at your next big party? Your local bakery may make some up for you if you order a few dozen buns.

A trick I sometimes use when I'm time-poor, is to use a cookie cutter to cut out bread buns from larger pieces of bread. I'll buy some flat burger buns and cut out two or three buns from that bread. Or I buy a long loaf of focaccia, Turkish/pide bread or sourdough bread and cut burger buns out of that, using the cookie cutter. You can create a few different varieties of bread buns this way, which is great if you want to serve a selection of sliders at an event.

Brioche-Style Buns

1/3 cup lukewarm milk
3 eggs
2 egg yolks
3/4 cup butter, softened
3 1/3 cups all-purpose/plain flour
1/2 cup white sugar
I teaspoon active dry yeast (I packet)

GLAZE
I egg white
2 tablespoons water
1/4 cup of black and white sesame seeds (or just white)

Preheat the oven to 350°F/180°C.

Place the bread ingredients into a bread machine in the order suggested by your manufacturer. Select a dough cycle.

Turn finished dough out onto a lightly floured board and knead for 2–3 minutes. Place in a greased bowl, cover with cling wrap and let rise for 1 hour. The dough should double in size.

Punch down the dough and separate into 15–24 balls/buns. Place onto a baking parchment/paper-lined baking tray with about 3/4 in/2 cm between each bun. Cover with cling wrap and set aside to rise in a warm place until doubled in size.

Whisk together 1 egg white and the water. Brush onto the top of the buns. Sprinkle with black and white sesame seeds.

Bake in the preheated oven until golden brown, about 15–18 minutes.

These French-style bread buns are great with any burger but is a must-have with the Wagyu Beef on a Brioche Bun. After making these buns you will never want to make anything but brioche buns for your sliders.

crusty soft buns

1–2 tablespoons butter, melted
1 egg
1 cup milk
12 oz/520 g all-purpose/plain flour
1 teaspoon salt
1 teaspoon active dried yeast (1 packet)

GLAZE
1 tablespoon butter, melted, or 1 egg white
¼ cup water
¼ cup sesame seeds

In a bowl, whisk together the melted butter, egg and milk. Place the flour, salt and yeast and the egg milk mixture in the bread maker. Select a cycle as per your machine manufacturer's instructions. Run the mix cycle.

When the cycle has finished the mixing, turn out the dough onto a lightly floured surface. Roll the dough to ½ in/1–1.5 cm thickness. Using a 2 in/5 cm cookie cutter cut circles in the dough, cutting the dough close together to get as many buns as possible. Roll the scraps together and let rest for 10–15 minutes then roll and cut again.

Lay the buns out on a baking tray covered with baking parchment/paper, spacing the buns about ¾ in/2 cm apart. Cover the buns with a tea towel and let rise until double in size, about 40 minutes. They will not rise that high but we don't want the rolls to be tall like dinner rolls. Preheat the oven to 375°F/190°C.

Brush the buns with butter to give a soft, light golden crust or the egg water mix to give a shiny dark crust and sprinkle with the sesame seeds. Bake for 12 to 18 minutes until golden brown. Cool the buns on a rack.

Note: Rise time is only a guide as many factors are in play, such as how you kneaded the dough, what yeast you used, so the dough may not double in size during the amount of time indicated.

Another way to make the buns, if you don't have a cookie cutter, is to roll the dough into a 2 in/5 cm log and slice the log into ½ in/1–1.5 cm discs and gently shape the buns.

Use the pizza dough setting on bread maker to mix your dough but don't bake.

Hamburger buns (gluten-free)

2 tablespoons gelatine
2 teaspoons sugar
2 teaspoons salt
1 lb/500g Superfine Flour Mix (see recipe)
2 tablespoons dried yeast
3 egg whites
½ teaspoon citric acid
½ cup olive oil

GLAZE
1 tablespoon butter, melted, or 1 egg white
¼ cup water
¼ cup sesame seeds

Preheat the oven to 400°F/200°C. Grease three heavy pudding trays with margarine. Place 2 cups of cold water into a large mixing bowl and add the gelatine, sugar and salt. Stand for 2 minutes to soften the gelatine. Heat the gelatine mixture for approximately 1 minute until clear. Add the flour and yeast to the warm liquid and beat with an electric mixer for about 1 minute.

Cover the bowl with a large plastic bag. Leave to rise for 10 minutes. Whisk the egg whites and citric acid in a separate bowl until stiff. Add the beaten egg whites and oil to the bread mixture and beat for about 2 minutes.

Separate into 12–16 balls/buns. Place onto a baking tray lined with baking parchment/paper with about ¾ in/2 cm between each bun. Cover with cling wrap and set aside to rise in a warm place until doubled in size. Brush the buns with butter to give a soft, light golden crust or the egg water mix for a shiny dark crust. Bake for 12 to 18 minutes until golden brown. Cool the buns on a rack.

superfine flour mix

7 oz/200 g besan flour (made from ground
   chickpeas/garbanzo beans and is pale yellow
   in colour)
7 oz/200 g potato starch

5 oz/150 g tapioca starch
3½ oz/100 g fine rice flour

Weigh the ingredients, place them in a large plastic bag and shake well. Sieve into another
bag and shake again.

Sliders

Breakfast Sliders

8 eggs
salt and pepper, to taste
1 tablespoon butter
12 rashers bacon

12 small hash browns
barbecue sauce, to serve
12 wholemeal slider buns

In a bowl, beat the eggs and ¼ cup cold water until combined. Season with salt and pepper.

In a medium non-stick frying pan, heat the butter over a medium-high heat. Once the butter is foaming, add the beaten eggs. Tilt the frying pan to cover the entire frying pan, using a spatula to drag the cooked egg from the outside to the middle of the pan. The omelette should be about ¾ in/2 cm thick. Place the pan under a broiler or grill on medium-high to brown the top of the omelette lightly. Remove from pan and lay flat on a plate or chopping board.

Cut the bacon slices to fit the buns and cook in a frying pan or under the grill until crispy. Bake the hash browns as per the packet instructions. Using a cookie cutter cut out the cooked omelette to fit the buns.

Slice the buns in half lengthways.

To assemble your sliders, add a circle of omelette, a piece of cooked bacon, some barbecue sauce, then a hash brown on top of the bun. Hold it together with a cocktail stick.

The Classic Beef Hamburger with Cheese

1 tablespoon butter
1 small onion, finely diced
1 clove garlic, minced
17½ oz/500 g best-quality ground/minced
   beef you can afford
1 egg
1 teaspoon Dijon mustard
1 teaspoon Worcestershire sauce
salt and pepper

1 tablespoon olive oil
iceberg lettuce, sliced
3–4 slices cheese (Swiss or Tasty)
2 tomatoes, sliced
pickles
whole egg mayonnaise
12 slider buns of your choice

In a non-stick frying pan on a medium heat melt the butter and cook the onion and garlic until golden and allow to cool.

Place meat in a large bowl and mix in the cooked onion, garlic, egg and Worcestershire sauce, and season with salt and pepper.

Roll into small balls and flatten the patties to fit your buns. Heat the oil in a frying pan and cook for 2–3 minutes until firm to the touch or cooked to your liking.

Slice the buns in half lengthways.

Spread the bottom halves of the buns with mayonnaise, add some lettuce, a cooked patty, a slice of cheese, tomato and cucumber and the top of the bun. Hold the buns together with cocktail sticks and serve while hot.

Serve with tomato or barbecue sauce and pickles on the side.

chicken schnitzel sliders

1 cup panko breadcrumbs
salt and pepper, to taste
2 eggs
17½ oz/500 g chicken breast fillets, cut into
  pieces to fit buns
1 tablespoon olive oil
whole egg mayonnaise or onion relish, to taste

2 tomatoes, sliced
1 cup baby spinach
12 slider buns of your choice

In a shallow bowl, combine the panko breadcrumbs, salt and pepper.

In another bowl, beat the two eggs. Dip the chicken pieces in the beaten egg, shake off excess then dip into the panko breadcrumbs.

In a non-stick frying pan, heat the oil on a medium-high heat and cook the schnitzels until golden brown for 4–5 minutes each side.

Slice your buns in half lengthwise and toast.

To assemble your sliders, spread on the mayonnaise on the bottom half of the buns, add a piece of schnitzel, a slice or two of tomato, some spinach leaves and the top of the bun. Hold together with cocktail stick.

Add a slice of crispy bacon if you want. Serve with some potato chips on the side.

Beef Sliders

1 tablespoon butter

1 small onion, finely diced

1 clove garlic, minced

17½ oz/500 g best-quality ground/minced beef
   you can afford

1 egg

1 teaspoon Dijon mustard

1 teaspoon Worcestershire sauce

salt and pepper

1 tablespoon olive oil

iceberg lettuce, sliced

spanish onion, finely sliced

1–2 tomatoes, sliced

pickles, to serve

In a non-stick frying pan on a medium heat melt the butter and cook the onion and garlic until golden and allow to cool.

Place meat in a large bowl and mix in the cooked onion, garlic, egg, Worcestershire sauce and season with salt and pepper.

Roll into small balls and flatten the patties to fit your buns. Heat the oil in a frying pan and cook for about 2–3 minutes until firm to the touch or cooked to your liking.

Slice the buns in half lengthways.

Spread the bottom halves of the buns with tomato sauce. Add on a cooked patty, some lettuce, onion, tomato and the top of the bun. Hold the buns together with cocktail sticks and serve while hot.

Serve with tomato or barbecue sauce and pickles on the side.

DOUBle Cheeseburger

17½ oz/500 g best-quality ground/minced
  beef you can afford
1 tablespoon butter
1 small brown onion, finely diced
1 clove garlic, minced
1 egg
1 teaspoon Worcestershire sauce
salt and pepper
1 tablespoon olive oil

cheese (Swiss or Tasty, cut each slice into
  4 pieces)
hamburger or dill pickles, sliced
your choice of condiments
12 slider buns of your choice

Finely dice the onion and garlic, sweat in butter until golden and allow to cool. Place mince in a large bowl combine with onion, garlic, egg and Worcestershire sauce and season to taste.

Roll into small balls and flatten the patties to fit your buns. Heat the oil and cook the patties for 2–3 minutes for well done or until cooked to your liking.

Remove the patties from the pan and place onto a plate. Add a slice of cheese then another patty then another slice of cheese and leave for the cheese to melt.

Slice your buns in half lengthways.

Add the cooked double cheeseburger patty, top with a slice or two of pickles and your choice of condiments. Put the top bun on and hold the sliders together with a cocktail stick.

Serve this with some classic beer-battered fries or potato salad.

Chicken and bacon
Club Sliders

17½ oz/500 g ground/minced chicken
½ cup dried breadcrumbs
1 tablespoon milk
2 scallions/spring onions, finely sliced
2 tablespoons parsley, finely chopped
salt and pepper, to taste
1 tablespoon olive oil
12 rashes shortcut bacon
12 slider buns of your choice

whole egg mayonnaise, to serve
½ cos lettuce
4 roma tomatoes, sliced

Place ground chicken, breadcrumbs and milk in a large bowl. Mix in the scallions and parsley, and season to taste.

Roll into small balls and flatten the sliders to fit your buns. Heat the oil in the frying pan and cook the patties for 2–3 minutes each side or to your liking at the same time that you cook the bacon.

Slice the buns in half lengthwise and toast them. To assemble the sliders, spread the mayonnaise on the bottom half of the buns, add some lettuce, a patty, then top with a slice or two of tomato, a slice of bacon and the top of the bun. Hold it all together with a cocktail stick.

Serve with spicy baked wedges and sour cream.

Chicken, bacon and cheese sliders

3 skinless chicken breasts
salt and pepper to taste
1 teaspoon olive oil
12 slices streaky bacon, cut in half
12 slider buns of your choice
ranch dressing or mayonnaise, to serve
6 slices Swiss cheese, cut in half

Season the chicken with salt and pepper. In a large non-stick frying pan, add 1 teaspoon of oil and cook the chicken for 7–8 minutes each side or until cooked.

In the same pan, cook the bacon until crispy. Remove from the pan and allow to drain on some paper towel. Dice the chicken and bacon, mix together in a bowl and set aside.

Slice the buns in half. Spread the bottom of the buns with ranch dressing or mayonnaise. Add the chicken and bacon mixture and top each roll with a slice of cheese. Place the buns under a hot broiler or grill until the cheese melts. Add the top bun and stick a cocktail stick through the middle, to keep it together while serving.

Serve with potato chips.

Chilli Cheeseburger

1 tablespoon butter
1 small brown onion, finely diced
1 clove garlic, minced
17½ oz/500 g best-quality ground/minced
   beef you can afford
1 egg
1 teaspoon Worcestershire sauce
salt and pepper
1 tablespoon olive oil

3–4 slices cheese (Swiss or Tasty), cut into
   4 pieces
12 slider buns of your choice
bottled chillies, such as pickled jalapenos or
   chipotle in adobo sauce, diced
hot sauce, such as Tabasco or sriracha sauce
   (a Thai-style hot sauce)

Melt the butter in a non-stick frying pan until bubbling. Sweat the onions and garlic in the frying pan until golden. Allow to cool.

Place mince in a large bowl and combine with the cooked onion, garlic, egg and Worcestershire sauce, and season to taste.

Roll into small balls and flatten the patties to fit your buns. Heat the oil in the frying pan and cook the patties for 2–3 minutes each side, or to your liking.

Set patties aside on a plate and cover each one with a slice of cheese.

Slice the buns in half lengthways and toast them if you like.

To assemble the sliders, add a cooked patty to the bottom half of the buns, add a teaspoon of diced chilli (or more if you like it hot) then add some hot sauce if you want an even hotter kick. Hold them together with a cocktail stick and serve them while hot.

Serve with oven-baked onion rings.

Wagyu Beef Brioche Sliders

1 tablespoon butter
1 small brown onion, finely diced
1 clove garlic, finely diced
17½ oz/500 g ground/minced Wagyu beef
1 egg
1 teaspoon Worcestershire sauce
salt and pepper
1 tablespoon olive oil
12 brioche buns

whole egg, full-fat mayonnaise, to taste
iceberg lettuce, sliced
cheese (Swiss or Tasty), sliced
tomato, sliced
cucumber, sliced

Melt the butter in a non-stick frying pan until bubbling. Add the onion and garlic and sweat them until golden. Allow to cool.

Place the mince in a large bowl and combine with the onion, garlic, egg and Worcestershire sauce and season with salt and pepper.

Roll into small balls and flatten the patties to fit your buns. Heat the oil and cook the burgers for 2–3 minutes each side until firm to the touch or cooked to your liking.

Cut your buns in half lengthways. Spread the mayonnaise on the bottom half of the buns. Add some lettuce, a cooked patty then add the sliced cheese so it melts with heat of the slider, then tomato, cucumber and the top of the bun. Hold the buns together with cocktail sticks and serve them hot.

Serve with a side of beer-battered fries.

ChiCken Banh-Mi SliDers

¼ cup rice vinegar

2 teaspoons lime juice

I teaspoon soy sauce

I teaspoon fish sauce

½ teaspoon pepper

I teaspoon sugar

2 large carrots, julienned (thinly sliced)

I Lebanese cucumber

12 slider buns of your choice

mayonnaise

½ cup fresh cilantro/coriander

1½ cups cooked roast chicken, cooled and very
  finely sliced

I–2 jalapenos, thinly sliced

soy sauce, to serve

Whisk together the vinegar, lime juice, soy sauce, fish sauce, pepper and sugar in a bowl. Toss through the julienned carrot and allow to marinate for at least 30 minutes.

Using a vegetable peeler or a mandolin, thinly peel the cucumber.

Slice the buns in half.

To assemble your sliders, spread both halves of each bun with mayonnaise. Add some cilantro, a few layers of cucumber, carrot, chicken, a few slices of jalapenos and a sprinkle of soy sauce.

Greek Lamb sliders

17½ oz/500 g ground/minced lamb
I small onion, finely diced
I clove garlic, minced
I teaspoon ground cumin
I teaspoon ground coriander
I egg
I teaspoon chilli flakes (optional)
salt and pepper, to taste
I tablespoon olive oil

I Lebanese cucumber, finely sliced with
   vegetable peeler
tzatziki, to serve
salt and pepper, to taste
2 turkish pide loaves, cut into 12 rings

Using a cookie cutter, cut out rounds from the bread to create your slider buns.

Place mince in a large bowl and mix together with the onion, garlic, cumin, coriander, egg, chilli flakes, if using, and season with salt and pepper.

Roll into small balls and flatten the patties to fit your buns. Heat the oil in a non-stick frying pan and cook for 3–4 minutes each side or to your liking.

To assemble your sliders, add some lettuce to the bun, a cooked patty then a slice or two of tomato and cucumber. Finally, add a dollop of tzatziki. Place the bun on top and hold everything together with a cocktail stick. Serve them while hot.

These sliders are great with a Greek salad.

Lamb Fillet Sliders

I teaspoon ground cumin
I teaspoon sweet paprika
½ teaspoon cayenne pepper
salt, to taste
I–2 lamb fillets
I tablespoon olive oil
12 slider buns of your choice
3 small tomatoes, thinly sliced
I cup baby spinach leaves

I red onion, finely sliced
½ cup feta, crumbed
½ cup tzatziki

In a shallow dish combine cumin, paprika, cayenne pepper and salt to taste. Coat the lamb fillet with the mixed spices.

Heat the oil in large non-stick frying pan and cook for 3–4 minutes each side for medium or to your liking. Remove from the pan and let the meat rest for 4 minutes before slicing the lamb diagonally into ½ in/1 cm slices.

Slice the slider buns in half lengthways. To the bottom half of each bun, add the tomato, spinach, lamb, some onion rings and some feta. Dollop with some tzatziki sauce before serving.

Serve with a Greek salad on the side.

pork belly sliders with spicy caramel sauce

2 lb 4 oz/1 kg boneless pork belly
1 cup water
½ cup sugar
1–2 long red chillies, de-seeded
1 teaspoon fish sauce
1 tablespoon soy sauce

juice of half a lime
½ cup fresh cilantro/coriander
salt and pepper to taste
12 brioche buns

Preheat the oven at 420°F/220°C.

Score the pork belly skin at ½ in/1 cm intervals in squares the same size as the buns. Place the pork on a rack in a roasting pan, skin-side up. Pat dry the pork belly with paper towel and rub salt into the skin. Pour water into the roasting pan, enough to fill the pan to just under the rack. Place in the oven and roast for 30 minutes or until the skin is crispy. Reduce the heat to 350°F/180°C and roast for a further 1½ hours or until the meat is tender, topping up with water as necessary. Remove the pork and cut into squares to fit the buns, as scored before cooking.

In a saucepan, bring the water and sugar to the boil. Boil until it starts to caramelise. Add the chillies, fish sauce and the soy. Reduce the heat and simmer until the liquid has reduced by half, squeeze in the lime juice then set aside for later use.

Slice the buns in half lengthways.

To assemble the sliders, add a piece of pork and drizzle over with some caramel dressing. Top with a few cilantro leaves then the top bun. Hold together with a cocktail stick.

Serve with a fresh Asian-style coleslaw.

TURKEY SLIDERS

2 tablespoons olive oil
1 small onion, finely diced
1 clove garlic, minced
17½ oz/500 g turkey
1 teaspoon Worcestershire sauce
salt and pepper, to taste
4–6 cheese slices (Swiss or Tasty), cut in half
12 strips streaky bacon
12 slider buns of your choice

mayonnaise
seeded or Dijon mustard
12 slider buns of your choice

Heat a tablespoon of oil in a frying pan on a medium heat. Cook the onion and garlic in the pan until golden and allow to cool.

Place the turkey in a large bowl and add the cooked onion and garlic, Worcestershire sauce and season with salt and pepper. Mix together until well-combined.

Roll into small balls and flatten the patties to fit your buns. In a non-stick frying pan heat the rest of the oil and cook the patties for 3–4 minutes each side until brown. Place a slice of cheese on top of each patty for the last minute of cooking. While the patties are cooking, cook the bacon in another pan until crispy.

Slice the buns in half lengthwise. Spread the bottom half of the buns with mayonnaise, add a cooked turkey patty with the melted cheese, a slice of bacon and a dollop of mustard on top. Add the top of the bun and hold it together with a cocktail stick. Serve while hot.

Try these with some oven-baked potato fries.

Meatloaf Sliders

9 oz/250 g ground/minced beef
9 oz/250 g ground/minced pork
9 oz/250 g ground/minced lamb
¾ cup dried breadcrumbs
1 large white onion, diced
1 large egg
¼ cup tomato paste
1 teaspoon Worcestershire sauce
2 cloves garlic, minced

1 teaspoon chilli powder
1 teaspoon ground cumin
salt and pepper to taste
½ cup barbecue sauce
7oz/200 g Swiss or Tasty cheese, grated
mayonnaise or onion chutney, to serve
12 slider buns of your choice

In a large bowl, combine the meats, breadcrumbs, onion, egg, tomato paste, Worcestershire sauce, garlic and spices.

Shape into a loaf to fit the size of the buns on a baking tray covered with baking parchment/paper. You may need to make more than one loaf. Bake the meat loaf at 350°F/180°C for 35 minutes, brushing with the barbecue sauce at 25 minutes. Remove and rest for 10 minutes before slicing. Slice meatloaf thickly and serve hot or cold.

Slice the buns in half lengthways.

To assemble your sliders, add a slice of meatloaf, drizzle over some barbecue sauce and sprinkle with some grated cheese. Place on the top of the bun. Hold together with a cocktail stick.

Serve with a sweet coleslaw.

cajun chicken, avocado and bacon ciabatta sliders

17½ oz/500 g skinless chicken thighs
1 tablespoon cumin
1 tablespoon ground coriander
1 tablespoon hot or mild paprika
salt and pepper, to taste
2 tablespoons olive oil
6 bacon rashers

mayonnaise, to serve
2 avocados, sliced
1 cup arugula/rocket
12 ciabatta slider buns

Cut the chicken thighs into pieces to fit the slider bun. In a bowl, combine the cumin, ground coriander, paprika, salt and pepper.

In a shallow dish, lay out the chicken and drizzle with 1 tablespoon of oil then sprinkle the spices over the chicken and rub in well.

In a large, non-stick frying pan heat the remaining oil on a medium-high heat and cook the chicken for 4–5 minutes each side until firm. While the chicken is cooking, fry the bacon in another non-stick frying pan until crispy.

Slice the buns in half lengthwise and toast them.

To assemble the sliders, dollop the bottom buns with mayonnaise, spread on some arugula, a piece of chicken, sliced avocado and top with bacon. Place on the top bun and hold the slider together with a cocktail stick.

chinese-style Barbecued pork sliders

2 tablespoons hoisin sauce (Chinese barbecue sauce)

3 tablespoons dark soy sauce

2 tablespoons shaoxing wine or dry cooking sherry

salt, to taste

¼ teaspoon Chinese five spice

1 teaspoon chilli flakes (optional)

¼ cup brown sugar

1 teaspoon red food colouring (optional)

2–3 pork (tenderloins) fillets

12 slider buns of your choice

1 cos lettuce (or any lettuce you prefer), torn

2–3 tomatoes, thinly sliced

Chinese hot mustard, to serve

char siu sauce, to serve

plum sauce, to serve

12 slider buns of your choice

Mix the hoisin, soy, wine, salt, five spice, chilli flakes, sugar and red food dye in a shallow dish big enough to lay your fillets in.

Place the fillets in the dish and turn the fillets to coat. Cover with cling wrap and refrigerate overnight if possible or at least two hours.

Preheat the oven to 350°F/180°C. Using a roasting tray with a rack, fill the tray with about ½ in/1 cm water or enough to come below the rack level. Place the fillets on the rack and put the tray in the oven, cooking for 40 minutes, turning after 20 minutes. Brush the fillets occasionally while they are cooking with the leftover marinade. Remove and cool, before slicing thinly.

Slice the burger buns in half lengthwise and toast them. Add some lettuce to the bottom half of the buns, add a piece or two of pork to each bun. Top the pork with mustard, char siu or plum sauce and add a slice of tomato. Hold the sliders together with cocktail sticks and serve hot or cold.

popcorn Shrimp Sliders

½ cup cornstarch/cornflour
I cup panko breadcrumbs
salt and pepper
2 eggs
24 medium to large shrimp/prawns, peeled
   and de-veined
I½ cups vegetable oil, for deep-frying

½ small lettuce, shredded
12 slider buns of your choice

WASABI MAYONNAISE
few drops wasabi paste
¼ cup kewpie mayonnaise

Place the cornstarch into a wide, shallow dish and season with salt and peper. Place the breadcrumbs in a separate shallow dish.

In a bowl, beat the eggs with two teaspoons of water. Dredge shrimp in the seasoned flour. Dip the shrimp into the egg mixture, then into the breadcrumbs.

Heat the oil in a pan at a medium heat then deep-fry the shrimp in batches until they are crispy and golden. Drain them on kitchen paper.

Slice the buns in half lengthways. To make wasabi mayonnaise, mix the wasabi into the mayonnaise. Add more wasabi if you like an extra kick.

To assemble your sliders, add the lettuce to the bottom halves of the buns and top with one or two popcorn shrimp, depending on the size. Spoon on some Wasabi Mayonnaise then the top of the bun. Hold the bun together with a cocktail stick.

These sliders have a real kick to them.

candied bacon BLT sliders

12 slices thick-cut bacon
½ cup brown sugar
1 teaspoon chilli flakes
1 teaspoon ground pepper

mayonnaise
lettuce, sliced
2 tomatoes, sliced
12 slider buns of your choice

Preheat the oven to 300°F/150°C. Line a baking tray with foil.

Arrange the bacon strips in a single layer on the baking tray. Combine the brown sugar, chilli flakes and pepper in small bowl. Rub sugar mixture over both sides of the bacon strips and bake until crisp, 30 to 40 minutes, turning the bacon over halfway through the cooking.

When the bacon is crispy and sticky remove from oven and cut into pieces to fit buns then set aside
to cool.

Slice the slider buns in half lengthways. Toast the buns and spread mayonnaise on top and bottom bun.

To assemble your sliders, add the lettuce to the bottom bun, add a few slices of candied bacon, some tomato slices, then the top bun. Hold together with a cocktail stick.

Serve with a potato salad.

Ham and pineapple sliders

4–5 ham steaks
1 x 9 oz/250 g can pineapple pieces
12 slices cheddar cheese, cut to fit the ham
   steak

1 teaspoon olive oil
tomato or barbecue sauce, to serve
12 slider buns of your choice

Cut your ham steaks into rounds or squares to fit your slider buns.

In a frying pan, heat the oil on a medium-high heat and cook the ham steaks, turning until golden, about 3–4 minutes.

Slice the buns in half lengthwise and toast the bun bottoms. Place a ham steak, add a slice of cheese and top with some pineapple. Place the bottom buns under the griller or broiler until the cheese melts. Toast the top buns as well. Once the cheese has melted place the tops on the buns and thread a cocktail stick through the middle of the sliders, to hold them together. Serve with tomato or barbecue sauce. If you like, use sweet chilli sauce instead.

These will be a hit at your next kid's party.

cajun-style crumbed Fish sliders

1 cup breadcrumbs

2 tablespoons Cajun seasoning

1 cup all-purpose/plain flour

salt and pepper to taste

2 eggs

17½ oz/500 g firm, white fish (snapper would be good), cut into pieces to fit the buns

1 teaspoon olive oil

12 slider buns of your choice

mixed salad leaves

3 roma tomatoes, sliced

red/Spanish onion, finely sliced

12 wholemeal slider buns

aioli, to serve

In a shallow bowl, combine the breadcrumbs and Cajun seasoning. In another shallow bowl, mix together the flour, salt and pepper.

In a bowl, beat the two eggs. Toss the fish pieces in the flour and shake off any excess then coat the fish in the egg then the breadcrumbs.

In a non-stick frying pan, heat the oil on a medium–high heat and cook the fish until golden brown, about 3–4 minutes.

To assemble your sliders, cut the buns in half. Add some salad leaves, sliced tomato, onion and a piece of cooked fish. Dollop on some mayonnaise and place the bun on the top. Pierce a cocktail stick through the burger to hold it all together and serve while they are hot.

You could also top these with sweet chilli sauce. You could use Turkish pide bread instead of slider buns—just cut rounds out of the pide bread with a cookie cutter.

Bacon-wrapped Scallop Sliders

6 slices streaky bacon, cut in half lengthwise
12 large scallops, roe off (U15 size)
spray oil
1 lemon
12 small brioche buns

SPICY SEAFOOD SAUCE
½ cup mayonnaise (whole egg or Kewpie)
¼ cup ketchup/tomato sauce
1 tablespoon hot sauce (optional)
juice of half a lemon

Preheat the oven to 350°F/180°C. Line a baking tray with baking parchment/paper and lay out the bacon in a single layer.

Bake until the bacon is just golden but still soft and pliable, about 10 minutes. Remove and cool on some paper towel to remove excess oil.

Wrap a slice of bacon around each scallop and secure it with a toothpick. Place on the baking tray lined with baking parchment/paper, season with salt and pepper and squeeze lemon juice all over. Return the tray to the oven and bake for 12–15 minutes or until the bacon is sizzling and crispy.

To make the spicy seafood sauce, mix together the mayonnaise, ketchup, hot sauce and lemon juice in a bowl.

Slice the brioche buns in half. To assemble your sliders, remove the toothpicks from the scallop, place on a bun, add some spicy seafood sauce and add the top bun. Push a cocktail stick through the slider, to hold it together, and serve.

crumbed fish sliders

1 cup dried breadcrumbs
1 cup all-purpose/plain flour
salt and pepper, to taste
2 eggs
17½ oz/500 g firm white-flesh fish (snapper),
  cut into pieces to fit the buns
1 teaspoon olive oil
mayonnaise to serve
lettuce leaves

1–2 roma tomatoes, sliced
1 red/Spanish onion, finely sliced
12 slider buns of your choice

Pour the breadcrumbs into a shallow bowl. Pour the flour into another shallow bowl and season it with salt and pepper.

In a bowl, beat the two eggs. Toss the fish pieces in the flour and shake off any excess. Dip into the egg then the breadcrumbs.

In a non-stick frying pan, heat the oil on a medium-high heat and cook the fish until golden brown, about 3–4 minutes.

To assemble your sliders, cut the buns, spread on the mayonnaise. Add some lettuce, a fish fillet, tomato slice and onion. Place the bun on top and thread a cocktail stick through the burger to hold it together and serve.

Serve with tartare sauce and hot fries.

crab cake sliders

17½ oz/500 g cooked crab meat
9 oz/250 g mashed potato
2 scallions/spring onions, chopped
1 tablespoon parsley, finely chopped
1 egg
½ teaspoon onion salt
pepper, to taste
1 cup panko breadcrumbs (use regular
    breadcrumbs if you can't get panko)

2 tablespoons olive oil
12 slider buns of your choice
1 quantity Tartare Sauce (see recipe)

In a large bowl, combine the crab meat, mashed potato, onion, parsley and egg then season with salt and pepper. Chill the mixture in the refrigerator for an hour. Then form patties to fit your rolls and roll in panko breadcrumbs, pressing the patties in well.

Heat oil in a frying pan over medium heat until hot. Fry the patties until golden brown in batches and drain on paper towel. Keep warm in a low oven until ready to assemble sliders.

To assemble your sliders, cut the buns in half. Add some lettuce and a patty to a bun then dollop on some tartare sauce or sweet chilli sauce. Add the top of the bun. Use a cocktail stick to hold the burger together until serving.

Serve with tartare sauce.

Tuna Sliders

1 x 15 oz/425 g tinned tuna in brine, drained
½ cup dried breadcrumbs
½ white onion, diced
2 tablespoons fresh parsley, finely chopped
2 teaspoons Dijon mustard
¼ cup mayonnaise
juice of half a lemon
1 teaspoon hot sauce (Tabasco or sriracha)
1 egg

1 tablespoon olive oil
salt and pepper, to taste
1 cup mixed salad leaves, torn
3–4 tomatoes, sliced
Tartare Sauce (see recipe), to serve
12 slider buns of your choice

Combine the tuna, breadcrumbs, onion, parsley, mustard, mayonnaise, lemon juice, hot sauce and egg in a large bowl and mix until well combined.

Roll into small balls and flatten the patties to fit your buns. Heat the oil in a large frying pan over a medium heat. Cook the patties until brown, about 3–4 minutes each side and set aside on some kitchen towel to drain.

To assemble your sliders, slice your buns in half. Add some mixed salad leaves, a slice or two of tomato and the tuna patty. Dollop with some tartare sauce and add the top of the bun. Use a cocktail stick to hold the burger together. Serve them hot.

You could also serve this with sweet chilli sauce instead of tartare, if you want some extra heat.

Tuna and mayonnaise sliders

1 x 15 oz/425 g can tuna in water, drained
1 cup mayonnaise
1 onion, diced
1 tablespoon capers, finely diced
1 cup cheese, grated
salt and pepper, to taste
12 wholegrain slider buns
dill, to serve

In a bowl, combine the tuna, mayo, onion and capers, and season to taste. Refrigerate until ready to use.

Preheat the oven to 400°F/200°C. Slice the buns in half.

To assemble your sliders, add the tuna mix to the bottom half of each bun and top with cheese. Place on a baking tray and bake in the oven until the cheese has melted.

Remove from the oven, sprinkle with some dill and top with the bun. Place cocktail skewers through the middle to hold them together.

Pumpkin and Cilantro Sliders

6 cups grated pumpkin

2 eggs

2 onions, finely chopped

1 bunch cilantro/coriander, finely chopped
  leaves and roots

½ cup all-purpose/plain flour

1 teaspoon ground cumin seeds

salt and pepper to taste

breadcrumbs

olive oil for frying

12 slider buns of your choice

2 cups salad leaves, for serving

2 tomatoes, sliced

1 red/Spanish onion, sliced into rings

seeded mustard, to serve

Place the pumpkin, eggs, onions, cilantro, flour, cumin and salt and pepper in a large bowl and mix
to combine.

Roll heaped tablespoons of mixture into the dry breadcrumbs and form into small patties. Place patties on a plate or tray and refrigerate for 30 minutes.

Heat a frying pan on high, add 2 tablespoons of olive oil and reduce heat to medium.

Fry the patties for about 4 minutes each side until crisp and golden brown. Set aside on some paper towel to drain.

Slice the buns in half. To assemble the sliders, add a lettuce leaf or two, to each burger half. Add on the cooked patty, some sliced tomato and onion rings. Drizzle some seeded mustard onto the other slider bun and place it on top. Hold the slider together with a cocktail stick.

Spice up the patties with the addition of chilli flakes or add some sweet chilli sauce.

Rice and Vegetable Sliders

¼ cup brown rice, cooked
¾ cup oat flour
I small onion, finely diced
I clove garlic, crushed
I in/2 cm piece fresh ginger, grated
4 oz/120 g canned sweetcorn, drained
½ carrot, grated
I small zucchini/courgettes grated
2 tablespoons pine nuts, toasted
I tablespoon peanut butter

I teaspoon soy sauce
I½ tablespoons natural yoghurt
I egg white
I¼ cup dried breadcrumbs
I tablespoon olive oil
12 slider buns of your choice
mixed salad leaves
sweet chilli sauce, to serve
I lemon, quartered, to serve

Place rice, flour, onion, garlic, ginger, sweetcorn, carrot, zucchini and pine nuts in a bowl and mix to combine. Place peanut butter, soy sauce, yoghurt and egg white in a food processor and process to combine. Add peanut butter mixture and ½ cup breadcrumbs to rice mixture and mix well.

Shape the rice mixture into 12 patties and coat with the remaining breadcrumbs. Heat the oil in a non-stick frying pan and cook patties for 5 minutes each side or until golden and cooked through. Drain on absorbent kitchen paper.

Slice the buns in half. To assemble the sliders, add some mixed salad leaves to the bottom bun, then the patty and drizzle with sweet chilli sauce. Hold together with a cocktail stick. Serve with lemon wedges.

Wild Rice and Bean Sliders

30 oz/880 g canned soybeans, drained and
    rinsed
2 cup fresh cilantro/coriander, chopped
2 scallions/spring onions, chopped
1 in/2 cm piece fresh ginger, finely grated
2 tablespoon ground cumin
2 tablespoon ground coriander
1 teaspoon ground turmeric

1 cup wild rice, cooked
1 cup wholemeal flour
2 eggs, lightly beaten
4 tablespoons vegetable oil
12 slider buns of your choice
mixed salad leaves, to serve
sweet chilli sauce, to taste

Preheat barbecue to a medium heat. Place soybeans, fresh cilantro, scallions, ginger, cumin, ground coriander and turmeric into a food processor and process for 30 seconds or until mixture resembles coarse breadcrumbs. Transfer mixture to a bowl, add rice, flour and egg, and mix to combine. Shape mixture into 12 patties.

Heat oil on barbecue plate for 2–3 minutes or until hot, add patties and cook for 5 minutes each side or until golden and heated through.

Slice buns in half.

To assemble the sliders, place mixed leaves, the patty and a spoonful of sweet chilli yoghurt, on the bottom half of each roll, top with remaining roll half and serve immediately. Hold together with a cocktail stick.

vegetable sliders

14 oz/400 g broccoli, chopped
14 oz/400 g zucchini/courgette, chopped
7 oz/200 g carrots, chopped
1 onion, finely chopped
2 cloves garlic, crushed
¼ cup parsley, chopped

3 cups dried breadcrumbs
½ cup all-purpose/plain flour, sifted
black pepper
½ cos lettuce leaves
sweet chilli sauce, to taste
12 slider buns of your choice

To make patties, boil, steam or microwave broccoli, zucchini and carrots until tender. Drain, rinse under cold running water and pat dry.

Place broccoli, zucchini, carrots, onions, garlic and parsley in a food processor and process until puréed. Transfer vegetable mixture to a mixing bowl, add breadcrumbs and flour, season with black pepper and mix to combine. Cover and refrigerate for 30 minutes.

Shape mixture into 12 patties. Place on a tray lined with non-stick baking parchment/paper, cover and refrigerate until required.

Preheat barbecue to a medium heat. Cook patties on a lightly oiled barbecue plate for 3–4 minutes each side. Slice 12 slider buns in half and toast buns on barbecue. To assemble the sliders, place a leaf of lettuce on each bun, then the patty and a spoonful of Spicy Tomato Sauce, on the bottom half of each roll, top with remaining roll half and serve immediately. Hold together with a cocktail stick.

Red lentil Sliders

2 cups water
¾ cup dried red lentils
¾ teaspoon salt
1 cup onion, diced
½ cup carrot, finely diced
3 garlic cloves, chopped
2 cups mushrooms, roughly chopped
1 teaspoon dried marjoram
¼ teaspoon black pepper

$^1/_3$ cup dried breadcrumbs
1 tablespoon fresh lemon juice
2 egg whites
2 tablespoons vegetable oil
2—3 cups baby spinach leaves
mayonnaise or tzatziki, to taste
red onion, sliced into rings
12 slider buns of your choice

Combine water, lentils, and ¼ teaspoon salt in a medium saucepan and bring to the boil. Cover, reduce heat to medium-low and simmer for 20 minutes. Drain then set aside.

Heat oil in a large non-stick fry pan on medium-high heat. Add the onion, carrot and the garlic cloves and cook until onions are golden brown. Add ½ teaspoon salt, mushrooms, marjoram and pepper.

Cook for 3 minutes, stirring occasionally. Place onion mixture in a large bowl and let stand for 5 minutes. Then add the lentils, breadcrumbs, lemon juice and egg whites and mix together. Cover and place in refrigerator for 30 minutes to help firm the mixture.

Divide the lentil mixture into 12 equal portions, shaping each portion into a 1 cm/½ in thick patty. Heat the vegetable oil in a non-stick fry pan over medium heat. Add lentil patties and cook for 5 minutes on each side.

To assemble your sliders, cut the buns in half, spread one half with tomato salsa, add some spinach, a lentil patty then a spoonful of mayonnaise or Tzatziki. Add the top of the burger bun. Use cocktail sticks to hold the burger together and serve them while they're hot.

Serve this with a fresh salad on the side.

crusty herbed lentil sliders

1 x 15 oz/440 g can brown lentils
1 large white onion, finely chopped
1 tablespoon olive oil
4 large garlic cloves, peeled
1¾ oz/50 g parmesan cheese, grated
½ cup dill, parsley or cilantro/coriander
salt and pepper to taste
3 tablespoons milk or water
1 cup dried breadcrumbs

½ cup grated parmesan cheese, extra
½ cup chives, finely chopped
2 eggs
4 tablespoons oil, for cooking lentil cakes
1 cos lettuce, leaves torn
4 tomatoes, sliced
1 cucumber, sliced
sweet chilli sauce, to serve
12 slider buns of your choice

Drain the lentils.

Chop the onion finely. Heat 1 tablespoon of oil in a frying pan and fry the onion until deep golden brown. Add the garlic to the onions and sauté until golden. Set aside.

Mix the cold lentils, cooked onion/garlic mixture, parmesan cheese, herbs, and salt and pepper to taste, adding the milk or water if necessary, to loosen the mixture. Form the mixture into small cakes. Freeze the lentil cakes for 30 minutes to make them easier to coat. In a large bowl, mix the breadcrumbs, extra parmesan cheese and chives together and set aside.

Beat the eggs in a bowl, then dip each lentil cake into the egg and then into the breadcrumb mixture, pressing the crumbs firmly onto the surface. Chill until ready to cook.

Preheat oven to 285°F/140°C (to keep warm). Heat some oil in a frying pan and cook the lentil cakes in hot oil, over a medium-high heat until they are brown and crispy all over. Transfer the cooked lentil cakes to a preheated oven on a wire rack to keep warm while you cook the other lentil cakes.

Cut the buns in half lengthways. Add some lettuce, a cooked patty then tomato, cucumber and some sweet chilli sauce. Place the top half of the bun on top and hold it together with cocktail sticks. Serve them hot.

Felafel Sliders

3 cups canned chickpeas/garbanzo beans,
  drained and rinsed
1 teaspoon ground coriander
1 bunch fresh cilantro/coriander
3 cloves garlic, minced
½ bunch parsley
1 teaspoon ground cumin
¼ teaspoon cayenne pepper
2 teaspoons salt or to taste

black pepper to taste
1½ oz/40 g all-purpose/plain flour
1 cup sesame seeds
1 cup peanut oil, for frying
2 cups mixed salad leaves
9 oz/250 g tomatoes, diced
hummus, to serve
12 slider buns of your choice

Drain, rinse and grind the chickpeas in a food processor with the spices, herbs, garlic, salt and pepper and flour, mixing until moist. If the moisture seems too dry, add some water to the mixture as it is processed.

Shape the felafel mixture into balls about 2 in/5 cm across, roll into the sesame seeds. If you want you can leave them round or flatten into patties.

Heat the peanut oil and fry the felafel patties until deep golden brown.

Cut your buns in half lengthways. Add some mixed leaves, some Tomato Salsa, add a dollop of hummus or Garlic Mayonnaise and top with the bun. Hold the buns together with cocktail sticks and serve them hot.

For a change, you could get some pita bread or pide bread and cut out slider buns using cookie cutters.

Emaleigh's Chickpea Veggie Sliders

1 tin chickpeas/garbanzo beans, drained
2 eggs
1 tablespoon olive oil plus extra for frying
1 onion, finely diced
1 clove garlic, minced
1 carrot, very finely diced
2 stalks celery, diced
1–2 zucchini/courgettes, diced
1 teaspoon ground cumin

1 teaspoon ground coriander
salt and pepper to taste
½ cup rolled oats
½ cup dried breadcrumbs
whole egg mayonnaise
lettuce, to serve
Tomato and Chilli Jam Salsa (see recipe),
   to serve
12 slider buns of your choice

In a food processor, add the chickpeas and eggs. Pulse the mix to combine but don't over-mix—you don't want a purée.

In a frying pan, heat the oil on a medium heat and add the onion, garlic, carrot and celery. Cook until the vegetables have softened, then add the zucchini and the dried spices. Season to taste and cook for another 2 minutes.

Let the vegetable mixture cool in a large bowl for 5 minutes. Stir in the chickpea and egg mixture until combined, then the oats and breadcrumbs. Let the mixture sit for 10 minutes for the oats and breadcrumbs to soak up the liquid.

Roll the mixture into small balls the size of golf balls, then flatten to form patties.

Heat some oil in a frying pan over a medium heat and cook the patties for 5 minutes or until they are golden brown on each side.

To assemble your sliders, cut the buns, spread on the Tomato Salsa, the lettuce, then the top of the bun. Hold together with a cocktail stick and serve them while hot.

ice cream brioche sliders

1 quart/1 litre tub vanilla ice cream
grated chocolate or Milo chocolate milk
  powder

12 brioche slider buns

Take the ice cream out of the freezer and leave in the refrigerator to soften a little. Once softened, remove the ice cream from the tub onto a chopping board and slice the block of ice cream into ¾ in/2 cm thick slices.

Using a cookie cutter, cut out 12 discs of ice cream from the thickly cut slices. Place the ice cream discs onto a baking parchment/paper-lined tray and return to the freezer. Place the leftover ice cream back into the plastic tub and return to the freezer.

Once the discs have been frozen again, roll the outside of the ice cream discs in the chocolate.

Slice the brioche buns in half lengthways. Place the ice cream round on the bottom half and place on the top. Serve immediately.

If not serving the sliders immediately, keep the ice cream rounds in the freezer, until ready to serve.

Chocolate Sliders with Chocolate Sauce

1 quart/1 litre vanilla ice cream
12 brioche slider buns

CHOCOLATE SAUCE
2½ oz/75 g dark chocolate, chopped
½ cup pure cream
2 tablespoons brown sugar

Take the ice cream out of the freezer and leave in the refrigerator to soften a little. Once softened, remove the ice cream from the tub onto a chopping board and slice the block of ice cream into ¾ in/2 cm thick slices.

Using a cookie cutter, cut out 12 discs of ice cream from the thickly cut slices. Place the ice cream discs onto a baking parchment/paper-lined tray and return to the freezer until ready to use. Place the leftover ice cream back into the plastic tub and return to the freezer.

To make the chocolate sauce, place all the ingredients in a microwave-safe jug and microwave on medium-high for 2–3 minutes, stirring every minute, until the chocolate has melted and the sauce is smooth.

Slice the buns in half lengthways and place an ice cream disc on the bottom bun, top with chocolate sauce then add the top of the bun. Serve immediately.

variations

Chilli chocolate: In a small saucepan, bring the cream almost to the boil over a low heat. Take the cream off the heat and add in two halved chillies and set it aside to infuse for 5–10 minutes. Strain the chilli from the cream then stir in the chocolate and sugar, until the chocolate has melted.

Mocha: Add a teaspoon of coffee granules into the chocolate sauce after the first minute of heating.

Frangelico: Add 2 tablespoons of Frangelico once the sauce is heated and smooth.

vanilla sliders with pecan caramel sauce

4 oz/125 g butter
¾ cup brown sugar
¾ cup cream
I teaspoon vanilla extract
½ cup pecans, chopped

I quart/I litre vanilla ice cream
12 brioche buns

In a small saucepan, melt the butter and sugar over a medium-high heat.

Once the butter has melted and the sugar has dissolved, add the cream. Bring it to a boil and reduce the heat.

Cook for a further 5 minutes until the sauce has thickened. Add the vanilla and pecans and take the sauce off the heat. Let it stand for 5 minutes to cool.

Take the ice cream out of the freezer and leave in the refrigerator to soften a little. Once softened, remove the ice cream from the tub onto a chopping board and slice the block of ice cream into ¾ in/2 cm thick slices.

Using a cookie cutter, cut out 12 discs of ice cream from the thickly cut slices. Place the ice cream discs onto a baking parchment/paper-lined tray and return to the freezer until ready to use. Place the leftover ice cream back into the plastic tub and return to the freezer.

Slice the slider buns in half. Place one ice cream disc on each bun half, drizzle with the slightly cooled sauce, then place on the top bun. Serve immediately.

sauces and sides

Tomato and chilli jam salsa

2 tablespoons olive oil
1 red/Spanish onion, finely chopped
2 cloves garlic, finely chopped
1 large red chilli, finely chopped
14 oz/400 g chopped tomatoes
10 sun-dried tomatoes, finely chopped

½ cup brown sugar
2 tablespoons balsamic vinegar
salt and freshly ground black pepper

Heat the olive oil in a pan, add the onion, garlic and chilli and cook for about five minutes, until onions are softened.

Tip in the chopped and sun-dried tomatoes and cook over a medium heat for about 10 minutes. Add the sugar and vinegar and bring to a boil, stirring every now and then.

Reduce the heat. While the mixture is reducing, season to taste. The jam is ready when it looks thick.

You can bottle the jam in sterilised containers.

Tartare sauce

1 cup mayonnaise (whole egg or Kewpie)
2 tablespoons gherkins, finely chopped
2 tablespoons chives, finely chopped
2 tablespoons fresh parsley, finely chopped

1 tablespoon Dijon mustard
juice of half a lemon
salt and pepper to taste

In a small bowl, combine all ingredients. Refrigerate until ready for use.

Halve or double the amount to make less or more.

oven-baked onion Rings

olive oil cooking spray
2–3 large onions
¾ cup self-rising/self-raising flour
2 eggs

2 cups fine dried breadcrumbs
I teaspoon Cajun seasoning

Preheat the oven to 440°F/225°C. Line two large baking trays with baking parchment/paper. Grease the paper with some olive oil spray.

Peel and slice the onions ½ in/1 cm wide. Separate the rings, removing the very small rings from the centre of the onion. You can freeze these for another time or use in another dish. Put the larger rings in a bowl of cold water.

Pour the flour into a shallow dish. Break the eggs into another dish and lightly beat. Mix the breadcrumbs and Cajun seasoning in a bowl. Remove the onion rings, one at a time and drain on some paper towel. Coat each ring in flour, dip the ring in the egg, then coat in the breadcrumb mix, shaking off any excess crumbs. Place the crumbed rings on the lined baking trays.

When all the onion rings are coated and on the trays, spray the onion rings with the oil and bake for about 16–20 minutes. Turn after 8–10 minutes to brown both sides. Cook until golden brown and crispy. Once cooked, remove from oven and place all the onions in a large bowl and salt to taste.

Always make double the quantity of these as they are addictive!

Beer-battered Fries

6 large Pontiac potatoes, cut into thick slices
2 cups all-purpose/plain flour
½ teaspoon baking powder

½ teaspoon salt
13 fl oz/375 ml cold beer
vegetable oil, to deep fry

In a large saucepan of water, par-boil the potato wedges until just cooked through. Set aside to drain and cool. Pat dry with kitchen towel.

In a bowl, mix together 1½ cups of flour, baking powder and salt. Slowly add the beer, a little at a time, whisking into a thin batter.

Coat the cooled wedges in the remaining flour and then dip in the batter. If you have a deep-fryer, fill it to 3 in/7.5 cm with oil. Heat the oil to 350°F/180°C and then cook the potatoes in batches until they are golden brown and cripsy.

If you don't have a kitchen thermometer or deep-fryer, heat up the oil in a large, high-sided saucepan. To test that the oil is hot enough, drop a potato wedge into the oil. If the oil bubbles, it is hot enough to start cooking your fries. Fry the wedges in batches until golden brown and crisp. Keep the fries warm in a low oven, until they are all cooked. Season with salt.

Use a bigger bottle of beer—then you can drink what's left over.

caramelized onions

1–2 tablespoons butter
3 large onions, halved and sliced
salt, to taste

1 tablespoon brown sugar
1–2 teaspoons balsamic vinegar

Melt the butter in a frying pan over a low heat. Add the onions and salt and cook slowly until the onions are soft and golden brown, stirring occasionally so they do not catch on the bottom of the pan.

Add the sugar and the vinegar. Cook for a further 10 minutes stirring occasionally until sticky and brown.

Use immediately or allow to cool and store in a glass or plastic container, in the fridge.

For some variety, add 1 bell pepper/capsicum, thinly sliced, at the same time as the onions. A great side to any slider.

oven-baked potato Fries

17 ½ oz/500 g baking potatoes
cooking spray
seasoned salt

Preheat the oven to 440°F/230°C.

Peel and thinly slice the potatoes, using a mandolin, and dry between sheets of paper towel. Line a baking tray with baking parchment/paper and lightly spray with cooking spray. Spread the potatoes out on the tray in a single layer and spray with cooking oil and shake over the seasoned salt.

Bake the potatoes for 20 minutes, turning after 10 minutes, until golden brown and crisp.

Try sweet potatoes instead of potatoes. Use a mandolin to slice the potato thinly but be careful with your fingers.

spicy baked wedges with sour cream dip

I teaspoon ground cumin
I teaspoon ground coriander
I teaspoon chilli powder
I teaspoon paprika (sweet or hot)
¼ cup olive oil
2lb 4oz/1 kg large potatoes, washed and
   scrubbed, cut into wedges
salt and pepper, to taste

SOUR CREAM DIP
9 fl oz/250 ml sour cream
4 fl oz/125 ml sweet chilli sauce

Preheat the oven to 440°F/225°C. Line a large baking tray with baking parchment/paper.

In a large bowl, whisk together the spices and oil. Toss the wedges in the spiced oil and then arrange on the baking tray in a single layer. Bake for around 40 minutes until golden, turning once.

Once you've removed them from the oven, season to taste. Mix together the sour cream and sweet chilli sauce and serve with the baked wedges.

Why not try sweet potato wedges instead? Or replace the sour cream in the dip with a mashed avocado for a dairy-free alternative.

Potato Salad

3 lb 5 oz/1.5 kg chat potatoes, whole and
  unpeeled
3 rashers bacon, rind and excess fat
  removed, then diced
¾ cup sour cream
½ cup whole egg mayonnaise
1 tablespoon wholegrain mustard
1 large red/Spanish onion, finely diced
1 bunch fresh chives, finely chopped

salt and pepper
hard-boiled eggs, halved (optional)

Put the potatoes in a large saucepan, cover with water and add a teaspoon of salt. Place the saucepan over a medium heat and bring to the boil. Reduce the heat and cook the potatoes until tender.

While potatoes are cooking, cook the bacon in a frying pan, over a medium heat until crispy. Remove from the pan and drain on some paper towel.

Once the potatoes are cooked, drain and set aside until cool to the touch. Quarter the potatoes.

In a large bowl, mix together the sour cream, mayonnaise, wholegrain mustard and onion. Add the potato and bacon and sprinkle with the fresh chives. If you like, top the salad with a few halved boiled eggs.

Use cooking scissors to chop the chives.

Asian-style coleslaw

1 red cabbage, finely shredded
2 carrots, julienned (thinly sliced)
¼ cup fresh mint, chopped
1 onion, finely sliced

DRESSING
1 tablespoon hot chilli sauce (sriracha is my
    preference)

2 tablespoons fish sauce
2 tablespoons rice wine vinegar
2 tablespoons lime juice
2 tablespoons vegetable oil
2 tablespoons sugar
2 cloves garlic, minced
½ teaspoon ground black pepper

In a large bowl, combine the cabbage, carrot and mint.

In a separate bowl, mix together the onion and dressing ingredients. Pour the dressing over the coleslaw and coat well. Refrigerate until required.

Add some peeled, julienned cucumber if you like.

sweet coleslaw

I small head cabbage, finely chopped
2 carrots, peeled and grated
I red/Spanish onion, finely sliced

DRESSING
I cup whole egg mayonnaise
¼ cup apple cider
3 tablespoons sugar
salt and pepper, to taste

In a large bowl, combine the cabbage, carrot and onion. In a separate bowl, mix together the mayonnaise, cider and sugar and season to taste.

Add the dressing to the cabbage and coat well. Refrigerate until required.

If you have a mandolin, use it to slice the vegetables. It will be quicker and easier.

Recipe Index

Acknowledgements

One of the greatest pleasures in life is cooking the food you love for family and friends and over the years I've done my fair share of cooking and entertaining, which has inspired the easy recipes that have come to life in *Sliders*.

There are several people to thank who've contributed to this book. Firstly, my twin brother John, the second best cook in my family. Without his help during the photo shoot I wouldn't have made it, even though I had to constantly remind him: 'John, read the recipe!'

To my enthusiastic editor Jodi De Vantier thank you, you made writing a book a joyful experience as did my designers Tracy and Keisha. Also, to the best girl in production, Olga, who can't cook but loves my pork belly sliders—lucky her hubby Terry can cook. Special thanks to the 'unseen' team at New Holland Publishers—Lesley, Tony, Marc and Jackie the general manager of Spank stationery. It might not be stationery, Jackie, but I know you'll love it! The sales teams across the globe, who will be selling my book, thank you.

To my author manager, Patsy 'just half a glass of wine, thanks' Rowe, guru and pocket dynamo, and her ever-patient husband, Dr Bill who eats everything I put in front of him!

To my Mum and Dad, which one of you taught me to cook?

To my very cool, and easy to work with, photographer Sue Stubbs, love your work. Thank you, I know we all worked so hard and I appreciate your support during my first shoot. And to Bhavani, my stylist, we did get there in the end, thank you.

Big thank you to a great bunch of friends, Irish John, Mal and Vicki, the fabulous miss Hilary Higgins, Simon and Kelly, Dave and Denise, Brooke and Marcus, Krystan, Max, Paul and Claire Reynolds who have all eaten enough of my cooking for a lifetime—don't worry Claire, I shall teach Sophie to cook.

To my wife, yes I know I talk about food a lot but I'm not hitting my word limit every day.

Above all, thank you to the booksellers for your invaluable support of *Sliders*.

Readers, I hope you enjoy this book. What started out as a bit of fun has turned into my passion and has added to my taste tester's waistlines. I hope you'll enjoy not only trying some of these easy recipe ideas for yourself but will introduce your family and friends to *Sliders*.

Eat, drink and enjoy!

David Cowie

Published in 2014 by
New Holland Publishers
London • Cape Town • Sydney • Auckland

www.newhollandpublishers.com

The Chandlery Unit 114 50 Westminster Bridge Road London SE1 7QY United Kingdom
Wembley Square First Floor Solan Road Gardens Cape Town 8001 South Africa
1/66 Gibbes Street Chatswood NSW 2067 Australia
218 Lake Road Northcote Auckland New Zealand

Copyright © 2013, 2014 in text: David Cowie
Copyright © 2013, 2014 in photographs: Sue Stubbs and NHIL (pages 70, 76, 78, 94)
Copyright © 2013, 2014 New Holland Publishers

All rights reserved. No part of this publication may be reproduced, stored in a retrieval system or transmitted, in any form or by any means, electronic, mechanical, photocopying, recording or otherwise, without the prior written permission of the publishers and copyright holders.

A catalogue record of this book is available at the British Library and at the National Library of Australia.

ISBN: 9781742574974

10 9 8 7 6 5 4 3 2 1

Publisher: Fiona Schultz
Project editor: Jodi De Vantier
Designer: Tracy Loughlin
Stylist: Bhavani Konings
Food photographer: Sue Stubbs
Production director: Olga Dementiev
Printer: Toppan Leefung Printing Limited

Follow New Holland Publishers on
Facebook: www.facebook.com/NewHollandPublishers